To the Studerschrader

Happy reading

Sally

11/11/18

Life...just life

ii

Life...just life

Sally May Harper

First published in Great Britain by Sally May Harper 2018
Copyright © Sally May Harper 2018

Illustrations painted by Joanna Ross,
pages 3, 18, 25, 57, 61, 69 and 88
Photos © Sally May Harper 2018
Illustrations © Sally May Harper 2018
www.sallypoems.weebly.com

ISBN 978-0-9956712-0-1

Printed and bound in Great Britain by Martins The Printers Ltd
of Berwick on Tweed in Timeless and on Offset paper
www.martins-theprinters.com

Book design by Rob Green
www.robgreendesign.weebly.com

Dedication

to John and June, my dad and mum,
from whose mould I came

Acknowledgements

In preparing this book, I have been helped by many of my friends. I am deeply grateful to you all. I would especially like to express appreciation and sincere gratitude to my mentor, the author Michel Syrett and latterly to Fran Campbell. Their suggestions comments and criticisms have provided a major support in making this book of poetry. My husband, David, has always been there for me and my children, Nat, Charls, Chris and Livs, well their belief in the possible is awesome. My family have been wonderful; a huge thanks to them all. I do hope many readers will use the wedding readings. I would also like to acknowledge the input from Rob Green my inspired designer. Also the original treatment by David Bradbury and illustrator Joanna Ross

"The unexamined life
is not worth living"
Socrates 399 BC

"I know I can reach you
high blue sky
I know I can reflect you
before I die"
Sally 1999

Contents

Leaving Childhood

Travelling alone

'Bliss'
that's the first I've said all day;
not a sound but a passing car
Sitting in a dry river bed
there is nothing on a par
with this
Lonely, not really;
afraid, a little but with maps,
car and money
that is security enough
There's a lizard friend
but it vanished
and an orange farm down the road
But there are mountains of trees all around
and I feel all around too
a part of this serenity
where there is nothing evil in me
just for this moment
But if I had to be here all day
and then another
would I still feel moved?
I covet these seconds
and now they've gone
I hadn't realised, thinking
I must be off, alive,
on the move again
and evil

© Sally 1978

Selling the farm

I had a funny dream,
the house, it really was burning
You had gone early, home
it was burning in storeys
collapsing in layers
the whole colossus red with energy

We went home
and saw it
burning, aglow and the earth so
still, while the layers fell

No noise came that we could tell
We couldn't hear you;
we almost seemed to have forgotten you
My father called, then left
I called but differently
you came

And now suddenly I was with you
a contact I had so long lacked
You coming to me and I turned;
a feeling I didn't know
and we watched the colossus as it burned

© Sally 1971

University love

In love I touch
but harm too much
I know you think
that when I blink
my heart has fled
to leave yours bled
but it's not all true
I think it's you
who have dulled my troth
by your unsalted broth
In all I do I wish to feel
happy, good and full of zeal
I cannot rue these days away
when wanting only a beauty ray
I know the ego I've debased
can even see the hurt I've raised
Here is life, its fire and fun
I wish to love before I'm done
to glow at sunset like at rise
instead alone my feeling dies
How can I start another
knowing it'll end like the other?
I want to meet a lover
who'll make my own heart flutter

© Sally 1973

Parental tug

If I were to forgive her before I die
I think my spirit would surely fly
Forget the hurt and misery
call it a part of my history;
perhaps she really did her best
Maybe this is my own test
to come to terms with unhappiness
and no longer make a fuss
because I could have done a whole heap
of things I never did. They'll keep
for my children. They'll have guidance for their goals
but will they have the pain to be richer souls?

© Sally 1999

Mum's garden from an open window

Early light is clear and strong,
gentle rustles stir,
topsey turvey blue tits
swing at their seeds

Cushioned in the country
from harsh industrial din;
butterflies rest boldly
on flowers in Van Gogh bloom

Simple not ironed smart,
swallows no planes;
rustic in the garden: wooden bench,
wooden hoe, wooden tree

© Sally 2000

Our Twenties

Early hours

Alone now
I see him sleeping,
naked
Could I stay with him
for all my years
or would I yearn to tear
myself away, every row
making worse the tears?
The years of agony to come
fill me with fear,
yet now all is not foretold;
I just lie and wonder
Seeing him bold
beneath my eyes
I see we have no ties
Looking at his shoulders
free from me...
Don't be misled
by warm beauty captured
by dreamy drowsiness. I am torn
with these thoughts. I warn
myself take heed lest
this balmy bliss may at its best
turn sour. At worst kill listlessly
both of us. Fill us
with a lacklustre life
a day by day hollow strife

© Sally 1973

Betrayal

Betrayal
a word I fail
to square
I ban it
from my mind
A daunting word
haunting my tail
Has it occurred
to you I see another?
I bother myself only,
my conscience is lonely
I needed to do it
I couldn't stop
I cannot tell you now
I do not want a row
I can never tell you ever
It would ruin our hope
to be together
It's a fat lot of good
to think you would
understand
You would not
We would rot
apart

© Sally 1971

Reality bites

I thought I'd be relieved
when he said 'I can't come'
At the time I wasn't peeved
but how dumb I am;
for when the phone went dead
I stuck my face in the fridge,
couldn't stop, then a drink which fed
an inner moan. A physical ache
flushed over me. Bastard!
I think it's going to take
a huge effort to start another
thing tonight. I'm going to waste
the rest of the day
It all happened in such haste,
he didn't even want to delay
and talk to me tonight;
I've now got my own battle to fight!

© Sally 1979

Balanced thoughts

The haze, the stir
the crinkled heat
hypnotises my breath;
is it too hot to think?
Is there room to ponder
to link thoughts
that wander through the mind?
A kind of halting life
this sitting in the sun
The past is done
I want to shout
'I'll start again'
but it's too hot
Do I sour nostalgia?
There's time still
to fill the rest of my years
even though the fears
of tarring them all
fall heavily
on this sleepy heart
But when it's cool, the sun's gone
I'll start again
Stay time, wait a bit
I'll come too

© Sally 1980

A big 'do'

I could wrap a whirlwind
round this evening;
it wasn't a success
I went full of hope
now I sit and mope
on the waste of effort,
the bad taste it left
I talked to the wrong lot,
when I found the right slot
I talked rot
When I get dressed
I have these fantasies
I'll be the bee's knees
but mar it all
by a conduct too lean
I really mean to match
my manner to my dress
but I never do,
it's left as mildew on my sleeve
I just heave a sigh
as I lie on my bed
away from the night;
I'm always less than my dreams

© Sally 1984

Parting

The sun flanks this hillside drop with subtle hues;
nature so dense on the ground
the sky is left quite plain
Two white butterflies jostle over a wild flower
as I would play with you if I could
Is it beauty that pulverises longing
or yearning that heightens awareness?

I loved this land once
more than you;
the earth will last forever,
will wait for me while I cry

© Sally 1980

Self assurance

If I were somewhat sure of myself
his love I know I could attract
If my spirit were to beam high health
nearly nothing I would lack

For I know, you sage self confidence,
when you ooze from out of my pores
the world is at my feet and hence
his love is mine and he adores

© Sally 2000

Nature Always There

Jack Frost

Still here, night ghost?
You remind me of the persistence
of a snowdrop through hard earth
You throw your cloak
over the grass on bitter mornings
and are still here when the midday sun
stoops through clear air,
night created chilled charm
I watch you recede until you die;
glorious before the sun draws you,
darts its reaching rays,
licking, lapping around the edges,
pushing, poking, prodding,
right up to the hedges

© Sally 2000

Horses

Under an old oak,
back drop of dried grass,
three horses stand,
necks bent,
flies tail flicked
Unshod, manes uneven,
the sun strikes their flanks;
an image captured
and held by the heat

© Sally 2001

The Alps

Grey stone like a printing press
so solid it bruises the air
Once it was molten liquid steaming down
to arrive in towering compact peaks;
a craggacious mighty rock
Now years and years drift by;
time pushes our fate
and nightly casts our change
into wrinkles and then the end
but millions of hours just stroke your chin
We climb and conquer your stark shelves,
again no blemish on your rugged brow
Freezing nights you stand with the moon
Do angels on arched wing
circle softly your hardened crust
whilst we more fragile age in sleep?
Or do they play against your flank
and hear their fibrous wings crush?

© Sally 2001

The Thames

Refuse discarded by low tide on a muddy bank
where seagulls dawdle with no aspirations
like ours
The flat river walks past below a dank day
In jerky rhythms pigeons peck;
they and the Mallard ducks
look clean in all this dross
My day halts
as the ducks toss the cold murky soup
over their heads, quivering their tails fast
as it slithers down their backs
They emerge untarnished from the mire

© Sally 2007

Watching Others

Your fire

You scar me with your burning eyes,
your hands rise up and lift the flames
I stand no chance in this blazing heat,
know no water to quench your fire

Hips hold joggers low and distraught,
eyes are gaunt in their eager search
Not knowing if you'll stop at words,
the phone unhooked lies by the sink

You come for me with kitchen knife,
which later you swear was for your heart,
and talk of tiger burning bright
What mortal hand dare seize your fire?

What frames your fractured symmetry
when so overpowered with what's within?
Did he who makes the lamb make you
and know what furnace forged your brain?

I cannot have you sectioned yet,
I want your release from tortured fits
but in my heart's deep core I know
you'll batter my frame to pulp some day

© Sally 2005

Love in this world

I was fair in your eyes,
we had lovers' ties;
but my whims turned
billowed and blustered
I tear your heart when I scold,
my smile is there, but eyes cold
You bore me: love has gone
You roam the streets
from station to home
to think of a line
to give me some pleasure
but I am blind
to any treasure
you bring
I fling your warmth aside
I fire inside to tell you
your desire I can't abide;
the lack of love I can no longer hide

© Sally 1982

Redundancy

The early hours had him,
scuppered plans of deep sleep;
his castle moat had been planked,
his horses whisked from their stables,
in their departing tread his pride was flayed
The beauty of his day breaking
was dust in the wake of their decision

When he had asked her to marry him
life was a photo frame
In this his children would spring,
holidays mapped, their bed a flower cup
Now the bed cradled his worst dreams,
the frame held children to be schooled
Whilst her career surges on
their intimacy collides
with his definition of failure

© Sally 2005

Ill health

It slipped from our grasp;
wondrous sights to visit,
directions we'd ask
to galleries we'd saunter through
hip to thigh with you

Curious smells, exotic eyes;
laughs walking the streets,
menus from charming guys
different cities, another roof
wine bars on the hoof

Years paddocked with a wise eye;
retirement plump and saved for
splattered like a swatted fly
popped from its innards
when cancer bares its cards

© Sally 2002

Imagine losing a child

Raw pain
gnaws flesh and rips the chest;
carcasses fare better
hanging from a meat hook
The scorched anguish of loss
is tossed into the heart
that can take no more
or form any pattern
for a future
There is nothing
Soar, you soul
into the clouds
to take refuge
Sore oh soul
with this open gash,
no healing
you fair of hearts

© Sally 1999

Finding a Life Partner

Early morning swim

The soft body still satiated in sleep
steps into the morning pool
and Hockney ripples ruffle the surface
The velvet skin surrenders warmth,
intensely on the delicate inner thigh
The nipples, firm, paint the depth of the cold
as the secret of her nakedness
is made young forever by the moulding chill
Another day the broad shoulders of a man
push the water apart
His virility tight inside him, his buttocks frozen firm,
so that his muscles are carved now like solid stone
The water, moving quickly from his body, is louder
briefly than the cacophony of a dawn chorus
This swim is separate;
but the pool shower is seen from the bed
as it cascades from hair to toe caressing
After, the other draws the cold damp marble body
    back
into the memory of the warm sheets
to be taken with ardour by the viewing lover

© Sally 2011

Personal

Wanting you
so powerfully
to hold me,
take my mouth,
peel my pulse
from mine to yours
Love tongued longing
woven with wanton lust
Holding hunger high a little,
halting huge heaviness,
touching tenderly,
troubling to taste any trace
of yearning
Wildness whipped with caressing
placing penetration
through to our thirst,
desiring down to the dregs,
drenching passion
into our demands
Conquering the irreversible tide together;
reclining fulfilled, waiting the leak

© Sally 2000

Erotic wake

Powerfully carving the sea,
propelling a wake so prescribed
it whitens the inky water symmetrically
The launch sculptures the male desire

And draws her either side of him
lying on her back still fresh and playful,
knees flexed as the crest of the wave
smoothes to the fall
mirroring the silky inner of her thigh
As the swell slides up and breaks,
the yielding softness of her skin
is so delectable to his virility
She lies there on her back,
him kneeling, keeping his hard shape
poised over her,
up into the ruffles of her downy hair
he stretches to reach intimacy

When the boat slows
their unabridged ecstasy
peters out onto the white lace of the coverlet
spread over the water for them to lie on in their joy
until they subside together into the secrets of the sea

New Horizons

School years

Just a phone call at break
that's all it took
It gave my day a lift;
a kick start. I forsook
a weary heart struck low
from sleepless nights
and let my love flow
An unhappy day best
buried floated away
'love you mummy'
that's all she had to say
So they were worthy,
decisions she found hard to take
yet she would never know
were taken for her sake;
we must take a step together
with tiffs no heavier than a feather

© Sally 2000

43

Cricket whites

As he ran waving his arms
in farewell, splendid in cricket whites,
like a playful Greek god
dashing out of sight,
I leant on the wheel in delight

The essence of a boy,
the joy given in that simple scene
As he turned the corner, image gone,
I saw the future if never to glean
again that figure in cream

© Sally 2000

Growing up

Legs up to your armpits and bent lever
to your ear holding a lime green mobile;
laughing so that your white teeth nostalgias me
If mine were so, the flowers of my face
would blossom once again

Some nights how can I feel so blue
when sleeping still you move my heart
how can I love you
yet hate the angst it brings?

Uniformed but rushed entangled with those smiles;
buses, timetable, homework;
gorgeous smart in crisp shirt, hair scooped high;
whilst shoes not clean, trodden backs
Then sport 'til late, clarinet left assembled

as I grow old I love you more
if this poor heart could
but dreaming on I dread
those stony years ahead

skirt hung low and far too short,
too many goodbyes for my searching eyes;
calls from mobile ....no buses came
should I be there when she's told me not?
As I fall in love she's walked on out

© Sally 2006

Late teens

Pink clouds drop low;
kicking the sand thoughts drift to you
No one's left along the strand,
just bubbles chasing into froth
You say your hair falls out
Situations of nerves you walk in front
too young to avoid sharp orange bends;
you take life on with open chest
and fall just like a little child
The disco's green you stretch
those nights and push aside the days
Walk on, but brush and shine;
to blossom is life's full gift
Tread amidst the devil's red holes
but comb weak strands and walk your beach:
life talks to you in roaring waves
white bubbles play their endless game

© Sally 2003

'Sunflowers'

Girls, young and firm
yellow hope to the sun
no flopping as in the picture;
they want to reach the sky

Flung into the war of life,
bunched into a watered vase,
will they keep sure and fresh
until they wilt and age?

© Sally 1999

Moving on

He has gone now
and I'm drawn to his room, pottering around tidying up:
four earphones, three chargers; doesn't he need these?
His green snooker baize is his table these days
and round the smooth shining balls
neat in their triangle lie his 'things'
There are three sunglasses, deodorant, super glue,
odd socks, some dirty,
a red cricket ball, a new toothbrush from FX and what about
the big watch still on time from Istanbul?
Milk thistle he thought would help his liver!
Nail clippers, a bottle opener, sim cards, batteries,
oyster card and old train tickets
I tidy feeling his loss like wanting chocolate
He has left in the snow and we expect more
I would like to sob but am too excited for him;
he has left for Uni in a whirlwind, life ahead
I feel I could inhale a cigarette given up all these years
to assuage his leaving;
he will be 21 there and not here
Loss indeed it is, yet I could not have him here forever;
not forever;
that would be a handful too much!

© Sally 2010

Moments in Life

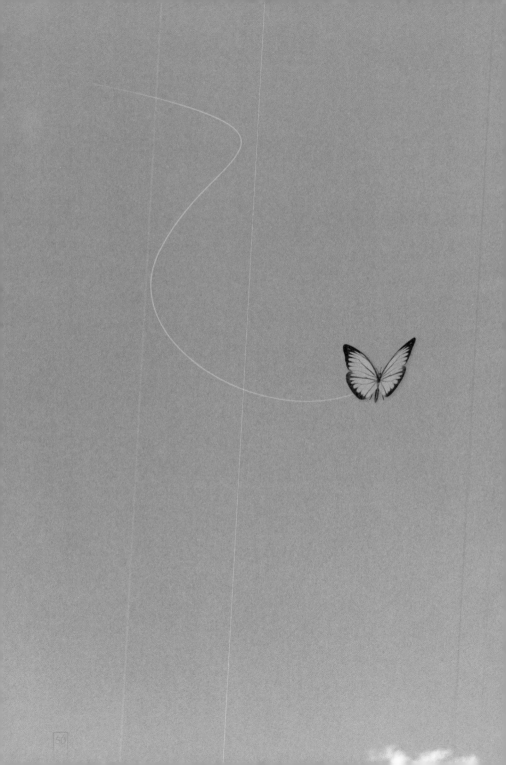

9 February

The marrow chilling frost
has gone, tossed aside
by an alpine day
hanging from a chandelier
Can this splendour suspended
give an eye to why we are?

I know I can reach you high blue sky
I know I can reflect you before I die

© Sally 1999

Nevada Falls

'Thirty minutes for picnic
and 10 minutes for sex behind that bolder'
that made him smile
Chilly damp on wet spines,
we trekked the final leg to the falls
and sat on a twinkling granite bolder
as smooth as a cow's bottom
where in the dark cleft the water cascades down
We had stopped briefly at Vernal Falls
but now, eagle high, bolder sitting
and sipping water, it fell
from his grasp to topple over as two Chicago girls
were perched the other side of the rail
I could not watch, they made my palms tingle sweat;
but they did not reach to grab
so I hoped it landed in disposable hands
Up there I thought of the mechanics of the world:
I could invent none of it,
but I did spy the spirit that drove it
as we hikers, drawn by such splendour,
arrived to inquire between firs and cedars
how the water falls to molecular beauty
On the descent I skipped amongst the stones
and sycamore leaves of gold and red
to relieve a bursting bladder and clutched
the little damp tissue to the end of our descent

© Sally 2010

A special chap

Dark skin against a grey day
illuminated by the shiny yellow jacket
of Richmond County Council,
he swept across the road
I looked at my pavement,
leaf free, not bad!
I called to offer a drink
and brought a steaming coffee with three please
'one day I want to be rich like you lady'
I noticed the tight short curl on his neck
black as the ace of spades and a wicked scar on the eye
I laughed and he added he would change the world
'here I work the roads and people rush, rush, rush,
with technology stuck to their ears.
They may be rich as sin
but it don't go with them when they die!'
I looked to retreat inside as the rain spat more
but remarked he was so right
'It ain't the world that is wrong, 'tis people
after they nailed Christ to the cross,'
he poked the green brush upside down in the trolley,
wiped his leafy hands on the bright yellow,
'I will go back to Jamaica when I am rich
and build a big house like yours
then I will change the world'

© Sally 2005

The soup of war: Loos 1915

I got late shopping, contents slung in panniers,
rain raining in ribbons as I tilted the bike to mount
and cycled off into the wet dusk
I remember the feeling: heavy droplets
peeling off my hair and dribbling down my face;
jeans slapped to my thighs and tarred there stiff and cold
So I imagined how it was in 1915
As the buses shimmered in the street lights,
true to an impressionist city painting
and lit my nervous way home,
I realised that there was no such mirage for them,
no arriving
No warm ecstasy after their black rain,
just filthy darkness
as the gelignited soldiers crawl
through a soup of blood and chalk
when ordered to go over the top – like 'my boy Jack'
with no iota of hope for success
Dirty wet, smelling of urine and lice, to be trodden on,
probably in the agony of dying

© Sally 2007

The hollow heart

The hollowed heart saluted shock and anger
but could not hail grief
He waited at the bus stop and his red body got cold
but nothing came, no relief
From across the road a little boy called
and told him his friend had gone;
he asked him in and the heart followed
over the threshold
He sat on the edge of the sofa on his pointed pink tip
and his hunched shoulders shook
as he stared at the patterned carpet
The boy took his hand and showed him kindness
and the naked heart looked at those truthful eyes
and when he left grief came and lodged with him
until he knew his friend had gone

© Sally 2013

A bunch of flowers

The soft light white
of a freesia flower
brought a smile of delight
and a change to my hour

It gave my heart
thought sad and slow
a sort of start
and a golden glow

© Sally 1983

Wedding Readings

Oh tell me about love

Oh tell me about love
Is it the soft touch when we share
or the fury of words as we flare;
do tell us does love care?

Oh tell me about love
Is it sun on a holiday bay
or stroking your hand on a hospital stay;
will there be love come what may?

Oh tell me what love is
Is it the soft fur of a puppy to cuddle
or swearing at a computer muddle;
make them all that little trouble?

Oh tell us about love
Is it a bright new model car
or butter in the marmite jar;
does love go that far?

Life was
Never Easy

Kitchen clean

Every day the mother wipes
the kitchen clean;
plans for new appliances,
dreams of modern units
He works, she saves,
she frets to choose,
takes time from home
selecting and processing,
tight schedules stress,
kids glossed, him shelved
Final installation hell

One weekend upstairs she sits,
a long look into the glass
Six months have passed;
it might be glamour
down below,
she has swapped a kitchen
to receive an older face

© Sally 2003

Shock

Heaviness heaped over him
huge hungry sadness caught him
utterly unprepared
He solidified
in a world of moving people

© Sally 2001

Where are you flying to?

Where are you flying to?
Take me with you
Are you flying to lands new
or a country known? Do
renew my hopes, guide
me birds. Show me a side
of life to soar above, tide
me over this depression, mind
my soul and find
a path tolerable
Take me and lift me up high
give me an incentive to try

© Sally 1999

The big bend

Don't be going too hard
on yourself at fifty,
there just might be another card
up your sleeve, though you may be
like the yellow dishcloth, worn and weak,
this is the big bend
No more chance of outer beauty, seek
instead the inner force. Lend
time to nurture inner love and dare
this to glow through a furrowed glare

Death, dangling dread before our eye,
halt him, hold him standing,
give you chance bye and bye
perhaps to seek another calling,
a new vocation for there's still
fifty years ahead, perhaps. Indeed
time to turn around and fill
a mind more mobile, lead
a healthy happy time;
old age fulfilled if not sublime

© Sally 2000

Pressure

I thought I had a grip
on today – just
Like slicing the end of an onion,
the hold is awkward, dicey,
it slips

The hell that is playing cards
in my head should be stopped,
but I can't get enough sleep
to get up there

© Sally 2003

The stalker

Stress like a stalker
tourniquets the brain
Close on your heels
it hounds you to earth

Hourly the problem hacks,
etching away youth,
lingers in the early hours
as fat lurks in cold water

After, the memory refuses
any acuteness of the agony
leaving the residue of stress
lurking in corners

© Sally 2003

Holding On

What next

All the lives we've ever lived
and all the lives we'll ever be,
tossed in the air and thoroughly sieved,
what use are they to you or me,
what use are they to anyone
when all is duly said and done?

All the lives we've ever had
and all the lives we'll ever be
stop right here and it's very sad,
for when we're dead I'll never see
your face, your smile or hold your hand,
we'll be no more than grains of sand

© Sally 1999

Beautiful?

All her life she was waiting
to become beautiful;
she felt it there, bandaged
Then the glass took a warning shot;
not only had she not arrived
she was going in reverse

© Sally 2001

Scarrabocchio

Only 'cos the wind picked up,
tossing the silver leaves against a blue so profound,
that I gazed up at those old olives
and a wondrous peace came over me
In your knobbly silver trunks would you walk in
and talk to me when I turn sleepless in my bed

You thrash and sway when turbulence hits
but calmly face the sun next day
and stand solid for longer than I will ever be
In contrast my body twists in human bedlam;
I am consumed by hours that seep together
You do not shed your leaves;
you have that inner beauty

When I walk into my earth's core
and along the corridors of my dreams,
a foreboding shakes which never meanders off
I come here to part the winds but am mocked;
I still come but must dig deep,
to save our children from brambles,
to shift the build-up of anxiety pasted to my trunk
No easy black head to squeeze:
it is all too deep, too dirty large
When the river is dark and fast,
where is the branch to which I can clutch?

© Sally 2012

How do I love you?

Continuous as light from sun,
only quieted in moon's slumber,
my love for you in chores or fun
is there just like the colourless air

But when we sat side by side
to hear that knell so deafeningly low
that your life clock and daily tide
will ebb away a little each day

my heart went numb as fingers white
I couldn't feel a single thing
On my knee your hand held tight
an image locked of that clinical room

Instantly now I crave one day
of how we felt before science spoke
to feel again just how we lay
as carefree lovers on time's strong chest

We will fight this lonely war
and give your life our one best shot
and then I know your heart will soar
above my ignorant passage here

Now and only now I can
express my love with open heart
before this day I think I ran
amok in fear of being hurt

This life is full of twists and turns
it moans, glides then it churns
now alive to how quick your wick burns
I'll try for gold as each petal curls

© Sally 2011

Snow

I want to lean on the gate and gaze;
snow pouts at me
balanced like ice cream cones on every rail
Then I do and hear the crunch under my arm
like cotton wool being teased out
and my elbow chills and dampens
My spirit can wander forever across these fields
yet the starkness threatens
'earth stood hard as iron water like a stone'
Cold bites but still I lean into the view
and my head turns onto my heart
How cold I have become
as the tussle to share marches;
the trees are dark skeletons for yards and yards,
are we two left with skeleton love?

© Sally 2013

Table and chairs

They were here our young ones,
here without babies
children for the last time
It's there like a frieze

A picture exploding;
I still see the surf
an echo of sea salt
on the Cornish turf

Come back to the present,
Yoga and Eckhart!
Believe in their wisdom
and give life a start

They'll have young ones one day
making new like the plough
such joy it will give us
to stay in the 'now'

Come here my dear garden
I'll smell a late rose
Yet sweet thoughts keep drifting
as a tear drop shows

So how do we do it
and often I try?
Oh Eckhart I read you
but fail to comply

For nothing can rid me
of a heart seduced
by this photo image
so clearly produced

Where chairs are all heaving
the table complete
the laughter I still hear
though empty each seat

That table is wooden
left out in the sun
makes stark to my soul now
that their lives have begun

Content to go to work
far from my care
too happy to quite see
my reach or my stare

But that's how it should be
and I will rejoice
though deep in my sub sub
I find this strange voice

A yearning, a longing
for those days in bliss
not often together
I still feel their kiss

So this spirit not shy
tosses the 'now' aside;
remembers the laughter
taking pain in its stride

There's beauty to cry so
there's joy in the pain
So I slip now from 'now'
to that spot again

No marks on the table
there's nothing to see
it's all in my mind now
my eyes are set free

It's only a mirage
that holds the chairs full
I stay for a short time
to indulge in this pull

Return cried and sober
to Eckhart the prof
my practice made perfect
my brain not yet soft

© Sally 2015

Feeling Old at Odd Moments

Wrinkles

Laughing, I meandered off to the loo
Sitting, I see the skin above my knee;
wrinkled more than any damp sand

As I walk purposefully back to the table,
I lift my skirt and curiously watch
just how those sagging wrinkles judder

I never noticed gravity winning
more cream; it matters!
It's all too late

© Sally 2012

A wondrous thing

A wondrous thing to watch a view
wondrous to hold in an open heart;
soft to carry when far away
and on return gives each day a start

The colossal beauty of its reach
even the noises seeping through;
colours transmute each changing hour
and the sea a band, a darker hue

Two hundred years our olive trees
hold the slope like a mighty foil
This bowl below will it endure
with the steady growth of human toil?

Clear air sweetens every chorus
spiced by a morning donkey bray
All fresh above the muffled rumble
as soft clouds disperse to a splendid day

Aloft two eagles glide and soar
circling pines on vineyard hills
Trees far darker than night shadows;
this land is strong no garden frills

I will take this vista safe in my heart
to years when age holds me still
and then in glorious retrospect
I'll recall those mornings and take my fill

And of nights when from a window
I would say goodnight to a view
Sleep well I'd call until the day
so hence I'll keep an old heart new

© Sally 2015

It's getting near

It's getting near
I feel your soft breath on my neck
Soon I am confident again;
different vitamins, getting up in the night
and not waiting for sleep to call
Yet the impression of that soft wind
chills my hopes for long life
I caress the months now,
they do not caress me
I caress my loved ones,
they open like an hibiscus flower
so here I will tread with joy
until you breathe more heavily

© Sally 2013

Just a leaf

They say it is lucky
to catch a leaf before it lands;
golds and reds upon the earth
Do you feel the hourglass sands?

Those leaves hold in the winds;
an autumn caress can't be fought,
by November you let go
I know how it is, not to be caught

© Sally 2015

What if life?

What if life is half askew
and what is life if all seems wrong
where sadly stress leaves far too few
times when you really long
for meadows, hills to walk along
or friends to share and make you strong

What is life if you give up
and what is life if you can't test
and see the half full water cup
can easily be more not less
Then you could raise that cup aloft
and take life on if hard or soft

Joy will never stop to bathe you
so you must catch it passing by
Put aside those rocks that slay you;
open the heart that's gone quite dry
Then snatching chances start again,
smiling with those who thought you slain

We are only given one life
tough and gritty though it be
So if you feel yours has more strife
approach the climb as a tree
Enjoy the spring leaves bursting through

(C) Sally 2017

and you will reach the sky now blue